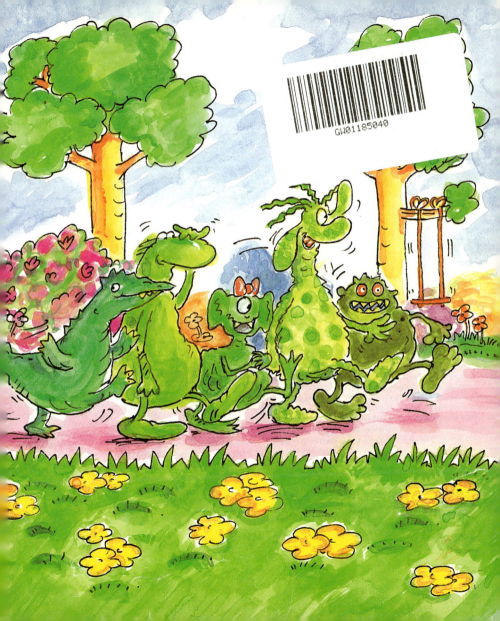

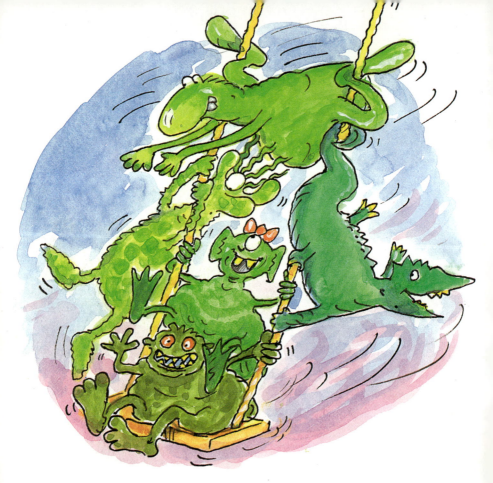

Five green monsters playing on a swing.

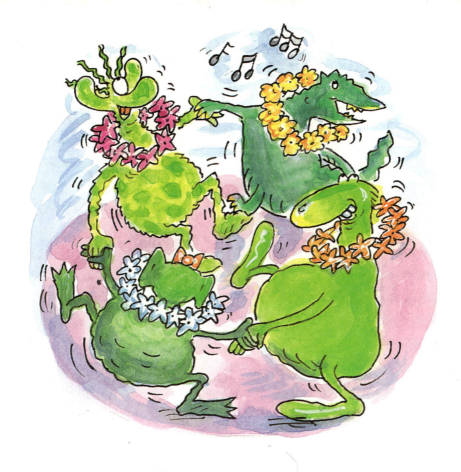

Four green monsters
dancing in a ring.

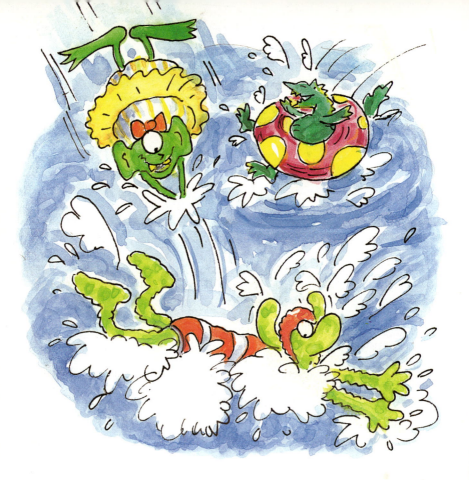

Three green monsters
diving in a pool.

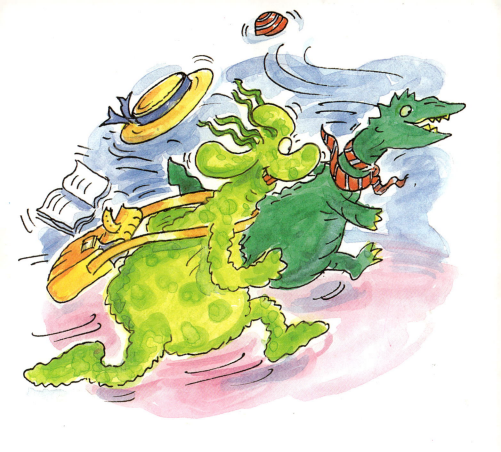

Two green monsters
running home from school.

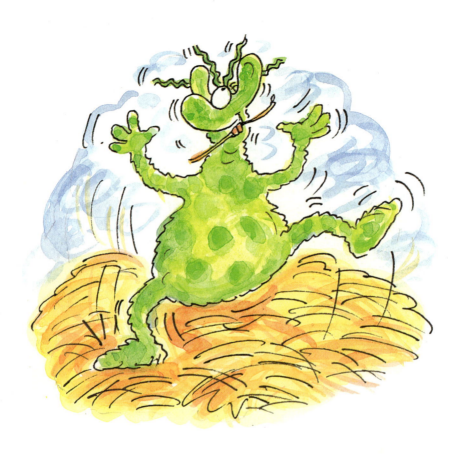

One green monster
jumping in the hay.

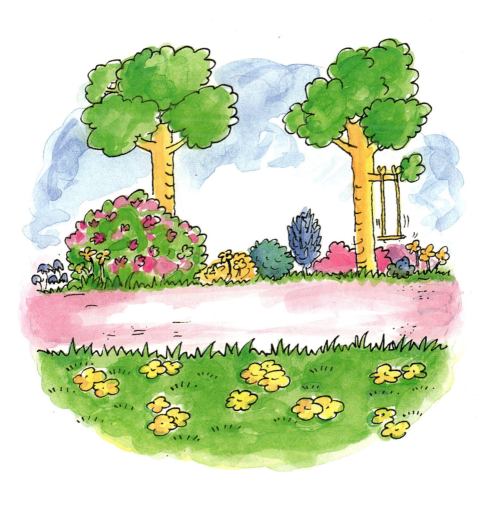

No green monsters left to play.

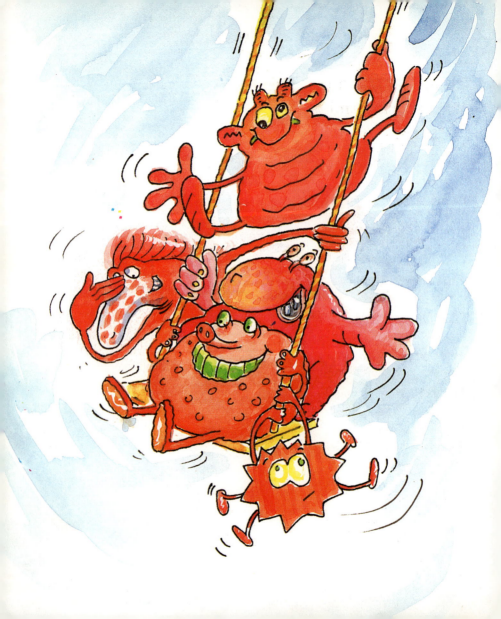